freefall

poems
by
Robert Medina

National Library of Canada Cataloguing in Publication

Medina, Robert, 1953-
Freefall / Robert Medina.
Poems.
ISBN 1-55369-589-5
I. Title.
PS3613.E35F74 2002 811'.6 C2002-902467-6

TRAFFORD

This book was published *on-demand* in cooperation with Trafford Publishing.
On-demand publishing is a unique process and service of making a book available for retail sale to the public taking advantage of on-demand manufacturing and Internet marketing. **On-demand publishing** includes promotions, retail sales, manufacturing, order fulfilment, accounting and collecting royalties on behalf of the author.

Suite 6E, 2333 Government St., Victoria, B.C. V8T 4P4, CANADA
Phone 250-383-6864 Toll-free 1-888-232-4444 (Canada & US)
Fax 250-383-6804 E-mail sales@trafford.com
Web site www.trafford.com TRAFFORD PUBLISHING IS A DIVISION OF TRAFFORD HOLDINGS LTD.
Trafford Catalogue #02-0402 www.trafford.com/robots/02-0402.html

10 9 8 7 6 5 4

CONTENTS

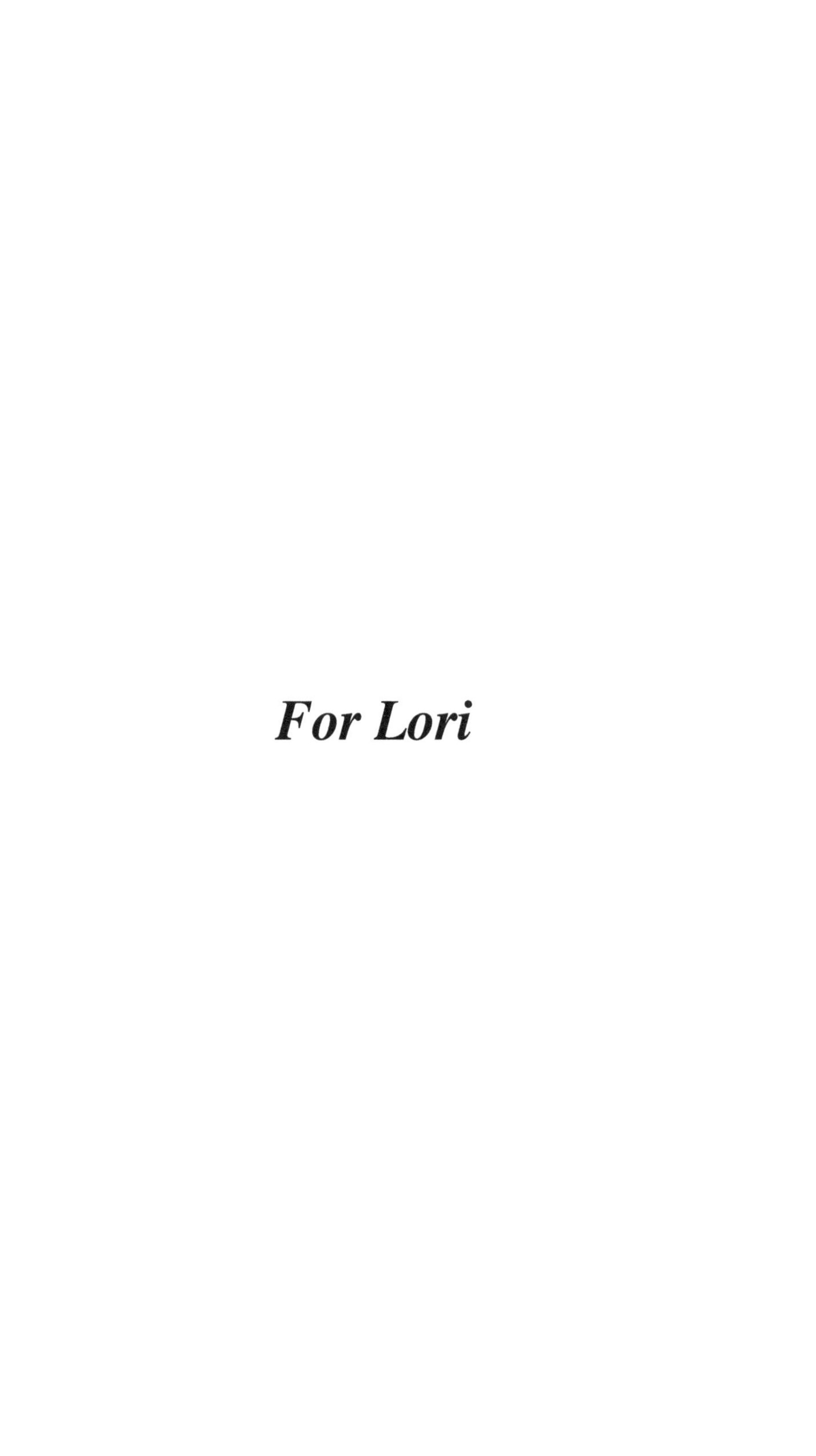

For Lori

A special thanks to Julie Cornwell for her continued support and guidance

Front cover photography by Marilee Southworth

Back cover photography by Lori Livis

Writer's Block

I knew that the words were in there
But it had gone so long unopened
My mind had since rusted shut
So I used my imagination as leverage
To pry it open free

The Weight of Words

The words I spoke
She then plucked from the air
And placed them on paper
Only to read back to me
Those very same words
Which my ears gathered up
And poured back into my head
So they had traveled full circle
Those seemingly light words
That had floated off my tongue
Had also left their impressions
Pressed by pen into the soft paper
Adding their weight to the thoughts
Of anyone who would read them

Fun With Alcohol and Cigarettes

Like a short distance runner
I sprinted through my life
Pushing constantly against the friction of time
Which slowly stripped away weeks and months
Eroding and peeling back the years
Until eventually exposing this old man
That was buried under all of those layers
Hidden not so deep inside
An old man that must now walk
At a very slow pace
Trying my best to slow down the friction of time
And save what is left of myself

Talk of Bora Bora in Tulane Hospital Emergency Room

She fed him whimsy for lunch
On which he gorged himself
Suckling to her tales breast
Nourished by the milk of her words
He gathered the strength to hope
That he too could pass together
With her the rest of their lives
In foreign places at seas end
Where the day knows no ticking clock
And the salt air smells of serenity
Where the beach winds long with ease

My Doctor Has a Pleasant and Relaxing Weekend of Golf

On Friday
He takes a germ of an idea
And screws it into the back of my head
Tapping into the darkest part of my imagination
Where he sets it free
Naked and afraid
To run blindly around in the dark
Refusing to turn on the lights
Until Monday

Sudden Death Overtime

Whose face shall be on the other side of the coin of death
I wonder as fate has chosen to flip life in the air spinning
That when it finally comes to rest in the palm of his hand
Is there even a chance in hell that I will have won the toss

Lies and Misdemeanors on Sol's Deathbed

Please give me shelter
From the words of pain

Or build me a porch
That I may retreat
From the fiery hail
Of wicked words

And if not

Bury me now in words of dirt
So I may live again
Somewhere without words

Five Questions I Want to Ask Ernest Hemmingway

Did you hear the shot?
Was it more painful than the pain you were already in?
Did it accomplish what you wanted?
Where are you now?
Are you there because God was upset that you came to the party early and without an invitation?

Moonshadow Deliverance

For reasons known only to us
The lone wolf cried out this night
His shadow thrown down
From a nearby moonlit plateau
All the while my own shadow cast darkly
Its rage upon the cold desert ground
Pounding silent fists clenched tightly
As I sat voiceless and very still
Staring up at the moon
Wondering why it ignored me
Why it ignored my wailing shadow
And that of the wolf
While the entire time
It was answering us all
Giving the wolf something at which to howl
And allowing my grieving shadow
A release for my pain

Cotton Fields of the Parish 1861

From my vantage point above
Looking down from the top hill
I watched their scarred fingers
Pick through the white sky of cotton
I saw their hands and arms outstretched
Flying through storms of thorns
Like miniature bolts of lightning
Striking out at their winged limbs
Hazardous flashes that surrounded
The billowy soft clouds

Forty-Eight Hours

Two days in March was all it was
Nineteen hundred and forty four
He was a gas station attendant out of Schenectady, New York
She, a factory worker from Pittsburgh, Pennsylvania
They met on that night through common friends
At this little beer joint that had music
And stale doughnuts on the bar
Overnight they were married
And within forty eight hours
He caught the train of war
Shipped out they called it
Shipped out with one bag on his shoulder
And a forty-eight hour marriage in his pocket
Thirteen weeks later pregnant and all
She got the killed in action paper
From a pimply faced boy on his bicycle
It seemed like a waste but really
Truth be known, it was part of something
Something no one would ever have suspected
Or would ever even know
He died a husband, father, lover and friend
Just as he had lived for those forty-eight hours
She went on as a widow, mother and confidant
Never having another forty-eight hours with anyone again
And the couple that got them together got divorced
Using up their lives with drink and fights

All those ironic years miserable with each other
The only good they had ever done
Was to put those two together
For just forty-eight hours
The only two people ever
To have absolute perfect love
And no one will ever know it
Not the drunkards or the bartender
Not the people on the streets or the battlefields
Not even the soldier and his wife
Two pieces of a very small puzzle
Torn apart by the war train
Two pieces that fit together tight
For forty-eight hours

9:30 A.M. Honey Island Swamp

I leaned back in my boat chair to watch the tall cypress tree
Looking like a man who was throwing his rather long
rippling shadow across the moving water
Standing firm rooted there up to his gnarled knees deep in
muddy swirls
With an old gray mossy beard swinging unkempt and
hanging
On long limbs outstretched as arms fallen open to wide
As though he was gathering up the good parts of the
morning stored here
And with the help of the wind that turned him toward us
He used his many brown fingers to point in our direction
Sending them gratefully our way

Man Came From the Suburbs

I thought about what they say
You know the ones that say
That man came from the sea
I thought of them
As I stood atop the skyscraper
Looking down at the river of heads
Flowing by below
Heads like waves rolling
Bobbing and rushing on their way
Draining out through tributaries
Called Canal Street, Poydras and Magazine
I thought of those people
You know the ones
I thought of them as the tide fell
When the evening came
And the riverbed grew still
Becoming a quiet dusty bowl of streets
Dry of the waves of bobbing heads
Gone back from where they came
Having rolled out to sea

Captain Meyers Comes Home from the War

There went the khaki man
Clothes pressed so sharp
They creased his skin underneath
Himself who once stood tall as oak
And who now is just as wooden

Carpe Momen

Stop
Grasp the moment
Pull it close to you
Let the moment melt
Then dissolve yourself into it
Become part of it
Warm and fresh
Swirl around in it
Then drink it down
And always remember how it tastes
For nothing in your life
Will ever taste that exact same way
Ever again

Two rednecks Talking On Canal Street: 1963

The idea now had two legs
And began to walk ahead
But reached an impasse
When it was just too big
To squeeze its way
Into their narrow minds

M. L. King of the Shooting Stars

He was the very last of his kind
He who illuminated a sun filled day
And added a star to the sky at night
Until the bullet came to touch him
And he passed exactly at the middle of time
And we knew that no day would ever be as dark
And no night would ever be again as bright
As no more stars would ever be created
But instead begin to go out, one by one
And with his, the end began tonight

Looking for God on Bourbon Street

Bourbon Street is the great old traditional bawdy show
Been there forever and a day plus a couple more I hope
And don't read me wrong from this cause I really love the show
But not only can you see just about anything there on Bourbon Street
You can also find about anything you want there too, including God

It's plenty stocked with large rotund barkers wearing tattoos for sleeves
While hawking their wares of sultry women and sometimes men
Pointing fat stubby fingers at first-timers and using gravel filled throats
To rumble out words akin to saying something like "Come on inside!"
Through their doorways darkened tunnels to sexy mystery tourist dens

Everywhere everyday people stream up and down the street jumping
Looking like fish caught in a net being pulled in starboard and port
Heads spinning about mouths hooked open agape surprised at all the normal ruckus

Doubting smiles on shiny faces hung there by Hurricanes and Hand Grenades
All the little fishes flowing upstream down the center of the midway

And on a lonely corner there is a thin man teetering on a narrow wooden box
Standing skinny black tie and white shirt soiled carrying megaphone in hand
Preaching loud and long winded about mans terrible sins to nobody listening
Looking like a cheerleader for God's football team behind on points rah rah

Farther down the long blacktop licorice strip treat street
Garter wrapped lace-stocking legs on a swing pop out from a window
While standing right below her there's a missionary woman
Collecting pennies and dollars to bring religion to a jungle
Somewhere other than this that she says needs to find Jesus

Across the corner from her is a man with a handheld homemade sign
Walking round yelling proud about the judgment day coming for sure
When all of the sinners right here will be damned to hell forevermore
All the while the taunting passersby spill warm beer on his holey tennis shoes

And hustling hucksters bet they know where he got dem shoes on his feet

Yes, you can find just about everything here on Bourbon Street
You can find flesh and blood by pound and pint full
And if you should just so happen to be looking for God
Well you can find him here too where he's been all along
Only now it seems he's just another part of the show

The Usual Madness

Set them in
Set them in deep
Your curved claw talons
Wrest them in my gray matter
Hold fast and cruel pulling
No matter how much I shake my head
Do not let go
No matter how I twist and turn
Hold fast
And you will be rewarded
Rewarded with the carrion of my mind
Feast upon it
Consume what little is left of it
Since most has been drained over time
Siphoned out gradually through the years
By way of many small holes
Bored there by your predecessors
With their diamond tipped beak drills
And their poking hard sucking tongues
Driven by incessant vacuous banter
They have taken most of it ahead of you
As I am somehow always the easy prey
Carried away willing by visions of the nest
Captured and held down grasped
By the slow torture of promised love

Four Years in Hell

I liken you to the sunrise
Whose long skinny fingers creep through cracks in the fence
And chokes dry the throat of already arid ground

I liken you to the sunset
Whose spine turns to face me yellow
And is seen as cowardice running away

I liken you to the sun itself
Whose flame brushed me once
And set fire my soul to ash

Apothecary

In the center of my heart
There are numerous little drawers
Each one containing
Completely different things
One is filled with remorse
Others with truth and pain
And still others with joy
And love and animosity
Which all slide open very easily
Except for that one drawer
The one holding forgiveness
Which seems to always get stuck

Shell Shocked

When I saw you tonight
It triggered something
Something that shot through my head
And just like years ago
I heard the bang
But I didn't worry about it
Because I knew that this time
I wasn't hurt
Remembering that years ago
You always used blanks

Clay Pigeon

You must have been wearing your pointy red ballet shoes
When last you tiptoed across my heart
Leaving painful tiny toe prints
In the soft clay
Which then hardened in time
Marked for a target
The clay pigeon
Shattered about the field

Friday 6:00 P.M.

The sun crashed down hard
Crushing the events of this miserable day
Squishing them flat
With the weight of the night
Reducing them into merely a smudge
On the fresh starched white shirt of the evening
One that tonight in the Chart Room bar
I will simply brush off
As just so much tired dust

Insomnia for the Recluse

Usually
I start out lying on my bed
Floating in the inky waters of the night room
Wishing that a wave would wash over me
And sweep me out into the deep sea of dreams
Usually
I try swimming frustrated across the blackness
Looking for the edge of sleep
Wanting to fall over it splashing down into
Some comfortable blanket to wrap up in warm and dry
Usually
I just continue to swim until my body grows weary
And I end up swimming all the way across
Reaching the shallow end of night where
I'm wading knee deep in the early morning light
Usually

Repercussions of Missing a Night's Sleep

I lost a dream last night
Somewhere in the sleep world
It strayed off from the rest
Then slipped into the nocturnal current
Where it now drifts along
Searching for that empty inlet
Branching off to lodge itself
In someone else's sleeping mind
For them to dream my dream
And wonder what it was about

City Council Meeting

Their tongues rolled out together
All at once
Then intertwined
Becoming a long red rope
Equivalent to tape
Wrapped around and covering
Sealing closed their own ears
Effectively silencing every other tongue in the room

The Mayor of Adjectives

We got us a mayor down here
Carries a thesaurus round inside his head
Other than that little book in there
I believe his big head is empty
Saw him in person last week
And I could swear the noise I heard
Was him giving a speech
But it turned out to be
Just that little book
Rattling round in his big head

One More Chance To Swerve

I know you tried
Tried to grab hold of my ear
With both hands
And pull it open
As wide as it would go
Sticking your head in and
Screaming into it
From the bottom of your lungs
VOTE FOR ME AGAIN
But I could not hear
For you deafened me
Four years ago
The last time
You grabbed hold of my ear

What's In a Name

We love to name things here in New Orleans
For some gone and others still living
Big buildings like the Convention Center
And little ones like Emeril's
Large parks like Audubon
And smaller ones like Brechtel
We name streets and even bridges
The long and the short
Named for all kinds of people
We're a funny place with funny heroes
So we may ultimately be the first place
To incarcerate a crooked politician
In a prison that was dedicated
And named after himself

...To Those Who Wait

I always thought
That I should wait
Until the right time
To give all of my love
Until it came to me
That now
Has always been
The right time

I Only Said Hello

The loneliness of beauty
Set aside from the ordinary
Its flawed tongue
Hides inside a perfect mouth
What must it be like
A paper-thin shell of beauty
Filled from head to toe
With pointy shaped sentences
That occasionally punctures perfection
And strikes out from pain
That I can only guess
Stems directly from
The loneliness of beauty

Natural Barriers

I see you often
At parties and events
We have mutual friends
In our seasonal circle
Those that know us well
Those who act as buffers
Like a dividing fall
Or the hyphened spring
Natural barriers
That make sure
We shall never meet
As the summer and winter
Will never know each other
Because of
Their friends
Natural barriers
Making sure
That they shall never come together
The way nature intended it

The Burden of Finishing Last

When in our favorite place
I asked why
And you shrugged your shoulders
Then
What had been us
Fell nonchalantly from those shoulders
Crashing to the ground

For you
A new life lighter
For me
A cold granite monument
That I must walk past
Every time
When in our favorite place

…Can We Still Be Friends

I wish
I wish I could have erased
Those words
Written on your lips
The ones I easily read
Before you ever spoke them

Love is a Quiet Heart

Lonely hearts beat
The same as those that know love
But perhaps just slightly louder
Hoping that someone will hear

The Last Will and Testament of a Poor Man

I carry many men
In my wallet
On paper and coin
All dead
And are reminded of their deeds
When I see their faces
And know their names out loud
They who were rich in fame
As I am rich in friends
People who will carry me
In their wallets
When I am dead
Making me wish
That I could have left them more
Because those will be pictures
That they cannot spend anywhere
Except to buy a ticket
To a memory

Advice on Death and Opportunity

When standing at Death's door
Do not knock
Better to pass him by
As he may mistake you for Opportunity

Marconi Meadows Murders

We were all of us there
Us being two children and myself
We three not knowing each other
But having the park and boredom in common
Till curiosity called out to them when
They spied a bird fly from her nest and
Capriciously using the knots as stepping stones
They climbed the thick-barreled oak across the street
To disturb the eggs resting among straw and string
Whereupon the outraged mother noisily returned
And chased them away down the guilty trunk
Then shortly after calculating no damage done her eggs
I watched as she pushed them by beak and wing out
Over the edge falling long to their end
To splatter upon the unforgiving ground
Laying out an evening feast for the ants when
It came to me seeming that for no reason
She aborted her children outright
But for her there was reason enough
That reason being the nature of truth
Better to have them go clean and unborn
Than fear for their future infection living
Tainted by the mischievous hand of man
Who can destroy any manner of things
With merely his simple touch

Meeting Lori

I sometimes think that luck
Is simply a temporary stand-in for fate
Which has taken the day off

Shimmer

When in our younger days
Thrilled I watched the moon
Wrap your face in silver glow
A picture for me to remember

And through our time of years
What your hair has collected
It has mined that precious light

Those silver streaks
Stolen from the moon
Now frame your face
With the riches of heaven

Exercise

The lazy days slip noisily away
Falling like dominos lined in a row
Creating such a racket as to wake me
Every so often
Early
Rudely reminding me
That I need to set up more dominos
So that I can stay in the game

The Cure for Cancer

His life paused
His heart skipped a beat thus
Losing a couple of seconds
Not unlike a scratch on a record
Causing the needle to jump
He missed an entire groove
A section of his life was passed over
And one can only wonder
What would it have been
What did he just miss
Perhaps the same old routine
Or instead
Maybe something special
That was supposed to happen
At that particular moment
Some inspiration
Some divine providence
Something wonderful could have
Just fallen through a misplaced hole
Lying around in his lifetime
So now maybe it was misfortune
Or maybe it was fate
Or maybe it was just blind ass luck
Stumbling over some bump in the universe
Aided by a gentle nudge from God
That caused this small portion of his life
To be lost forever

The only thing he knows for sure
Is that he will never know for sure

For Charlotte Raley

He took from her the painful noise
That fell taciturn from damp eyes
And traded from her the joyful clamor of life loved
While filling her instead with a peaceful stillness

But he gave something to him who remained behind
A perfectly clear bell like memory on quiet nights
While listening in the dark to the beat of his own heart
Knowing it would always ring out true
For it is filled with her special life

As Usual, Regret Arrives Late

Sadly
I wish I could
Have back every single breath
That I wasted in anger
And every single breath
That I wasted on greed
And every single breath
That I wasted on worry
So that I might
Have lived that much longer
Happy

Legacy of the Ashes

I will not lay there in the darkness
Waiting for the dirt to call
Waiting for the earth's tongue
To lick me gone like a slow sucker
Until I am all completely disappeared

I will instead be fed to the wind
So I may hide in the water and sand
In the mountains and rocks scattered
That the earth may spend the rest of its days
Trying to find all of me

Kaleidoscope

I have molded this shapeless existence
Into a long clear tube that started out closed at one end
Then began slowly filling itself with the remains of life
spent
And when it is full and seals itself off at the opposite end
I want you to hold it up to the light
And look at all of the pretty colors

Karen Wakes Up in Michigan

She cast off the slumber of years
Thrown aside like a heavy woolen blanket
Then sprayed on the new day
As a fine mist perfume
And in the roundness of time
She covered herself
With the scent of children,
A tranquil lake calm blue,
And the aroma of her quiet life
Gliding through the mist
While the sun
Attached itself to her skin
Giving her a glow of contentment
All the while loving the new day
And the way it smells

The Recollections of Cloth

As they took the wedding walk
Down a sun filled afternoon street
The wind pushed her veil
Pressing it against her smiling face
Bringing to the frail white cloth
An outline of her perfect features
Giving to the cloth a face of its own
Momentarily come to life
To look out upon the world
To briefly know what happiness is
And then relaxed again
Back into just an ordinary veil
But a very grateful one
That now and forever
Would hold one single memory
To have for its very own

Upon the Birth of Sami

From where does a man's destiny come
It is but carried to him on the legs of time
So tell your sons and daughters born
From one who once took destiny's walk
To be a footrace against himself
It will be delivered to he or she
Through circumstance lost its way
And perceived as a road divided
But it doesn't matter which road they choose
For there is no wrong and there is no right
Tell them that it makes no difference
Where either road eventually ends
Because end they most certainly will
That they should not consider the road at all
As it is only the journey that truly matters

Details

I must remember where I put the flashlight that I believe I used last when I was checking the attic for a roof leak that was spilling all over my tool box in the garage and wetting the power tools that I had just used to take care of a shutter that had fallen off the window. that was right before I sat down to do the bills that I often let pile up for lack of time and desire to deal with them. i must remember where I put the oil pan that I use when I do routine maintenance on my wife's car but first I need to fix the flush chain on the toilet that broke while I was trying to unstop the pipes right before I vacuumed up the water on the carpet that was such a mess. i must remember where I put the scissors that I used last when I was cutting out coupons before I placed the old newspapers in the pile that I must take out to the street before the recycle truck comes tomorrow which was right before I had to shop for groceries for Sunday dinner because there was a crowd coming over for the big Saints game. i must remember where I put the screwdriver that I used last when I changed an outlet that was sparking and that was right before I went to Home Depot in the cold rain to get one which was right after the light burned out in the lamp with a pop that made the cat jump up and scratch holes in the couch which I'll take care of later on as soon as I can find an upholsterer that can fix that sort of thing. but most of all I must remember where I put my life which I don't seem to be able to recall the last time I used it.

The Old Ladies Of New Orleans

Here in the Garden District
The homes sit as old ladies
Like rocking chairs paused
Stopping to look upon the passers by
Her bones are cypress rafters
With a hint of the rheumatiz in the joints
That creek as old bones do
And shudders in the wind
Like she took a deep breath chilled
Then relaxed on back to sleep
Wrapped in magnolia shawls
And if you look close you can see
Her skins of plaster dried and cracking
Which shows her age a bit
But often enough she paints her face pretty
Trying always to look nice for company
And like all stately southern belles
She stands solid on her reputation
With her feet planted firmly on the soil
And the heart of her rooted
Deep in the city
Holding it together
As roots naturally do
Keeping everything firmly in place
Despite constantly trying to wash her away
They are the old ladies of New Orleans

The most beautiful flowers
There in the Garden District

The Drowning House

When I turned on
A seldom-used faucet
The water came out coughing
Sputtering and spitting
As though the house
Were trying to speak
Through words
Caught in little bubbles
That burst
Letting out tiny gurgling noises
Then finally
A high-pitched scream
Sounding like a cry for help
As though the old place
Was gasping
Trying to survive
Just the opposite as that of a man
Who would have had water
In his windpipe

Sun Day Tan at Sandpiper Beach

It is a warm light
That bakes her skin to brown
Like delicious golden bread
That smells of aloe honey

It is a reflecting light
That brings forth the water
Beading up from her pores
Her body glistens
As if waxed to shine

It is the light of August
That brands her
The color of summer

Destin Sand

Those days at the beach
Got stuck in my head
As did the grains of sand
That I carried home with me
Picked up by my shoes
Sand that now lies
On the back floor of my car
Just as those days at the beach
Lay sprinkled across the floor of my memory
Lodging themselves in the crevices and cracks
That make up the loose wooden deck
In the long halls of my mind

She Always Looks At Me Funny When I Tell Her Goodbye

What I miss
When you leave
Is not only you
But you
Being you
Without you
Knowing what is so special
About missing you

Art Appreciation

I love the light that comes from your grin
I love the music that comes from your smile
I love the colors that come from your voice
I love the art that comes from your face

Wait

I had always considered myself to be stiff
Rigid in certain things but
Everyone continued to tell me that everything worth anything
Takes time

So I continued to bend without breaking
Never realizing that in the end
I would become so pliable in that one particular area
It would eventually take the shape of patience

New Orleans Fire Department, Engine 17, March 18, 2000

Lives pass through their hands like water
As they sift through eternity with license
Hoping to steal back a breath from darkness
Pulling it back to mix with a breath of their own
Returning life to the lifeless
With just the simple air
Of men who take away nothing
But instead
Always give of themselves

Beelzebub Plans His Day

First of morning drawn from the dark quiver
I will be the arrow that pierces the heart of God
The one that brings pain to the painless
Hopelessness to the hopeful
And opportunity to the desperate
I will watch him fall wounded
Only to rise again healed and vengeful
But it matters not to me
For I will seduce him to pain again through you…
Right after lunch

A Westbank Nursing Home, 3:02 A.M.

They had all started out as large rocks
Who faced each new day standing
Hard and impervious invincible
Until the wind and rain steadily
Chipped away their young surface
And wore them down in size smooth
Reducing them to porous little pebbles
In the shoes of their children

The Death of the Widower Hornsby

When the rich man dies, I shed no tears
For I know the gold he saved will be spent
By those that need it least

And when a powerful man dies, I feel no remorse
For I know the favors he stored will not be lost
To he that takes his place

But when a lonely man dies, I mourn hard
For no one knows what happens
To the lonely man's love gone unused

A Full Life Empty

He was a hard shell of a man
That was easy to see
Calloused outside by a harsh and harried life
Where his dark stare drove away
Any hope of delivery to kindness
From anyone who could possibly care
Sharing his lonely thoughts with no one
Until he eventually died
Thus drawing forth the last tear
That he would ever shed
Which hung clinging
From the corner of his eye
A solitary tear
Filled with his final thoughts
And his final anguish
And I'm sure his final pain
One last tear
Which reflected his passing
And was held intact by a transparent skin
A tight surface that kept his last feelings in place
But was unlike the tough skin he showed us in life
Because in the end
One could see right through him

Twelve Hours In Woodlawn Cemetery

On January fourteenth at sunrise
I watched the shadows of the dead
Push their way to the surface
Slowly revealing themselves as they
Held clinging onto the gravestones
That anchored them to their places
Gradually moving across the ground
They showed themselves to me all day
But traveled at such a pace
That I scarcely noticed
While I sat there grieving and watching
Searching for any sign to sense of it all
Spending twelve hours in a cemetery
Brought me to know that
The shadows of the dead are cast everyday
Moving right before our very eyes
If we would just take the time to look, I thought
As I watched them slip back to their rest
On January fourteenth at sunset

Pilot's Prayer

O Ye gods of my ancient people
Take me to the high place
Prop me up on your shoulders
So that I may rub my head
On the ceiling of Olympus
Carried around as victor
To cheers so loud and fierce
That the walls will crumble
Falling down around us
Burying you all gods but one
Who catches me in soft hands
And places me back lightly safe to earth
Leaving behind the false vanquished
That I may know only him
As my one true savior

Pearls of Wisdom

Years ago I met a haggard man with twisted gray curls in his hair
A couple of gold teeth shining and smiling at me from across the counter
His hands rough and hard tested but with a gentle touch to his work
We talked a lot when he wasn't joking with the other customers
He said he'd been shucking oysters for about fifty-seven years
Right there in the Quarter almost his whole life shucking oysters
Said he never did anything else and never wanted to
He told me that he had lived here since he was just a little baby
Told me too that he had never been out of the city except once
When he went to a wedding for his son in Biloxi, Mississippi
One day we got to talking like we usually did and he told me something else
He said that he didn't sleep much but when he did sleep he never dreamed
Never could recall ever in his whole life having one single dream
I thought that was peculiar until I began to watch him closer

Standing there laughing and cuttin' up with everybody that came in the door
Whistling and singing and having a good old time every afternoon
Happy with himself and happy with the life he'd made
And I realized then that maybe some people don't need to dream
And I envied him

Movement in E Major

For I love where the music takes me
As I sat there on the marble floor
Eyes closed and listening intently
Holding my breath by nervous straps
When the first note was struck
High up on the piano
One long single spirited note
That came my way and I hitched on
Pulling myself up and onto it
Riding it bareback smooth through the air
Determined to stay on as long as it could sustain
Till I would wear it down listening
The note carrying me off a long way
Until it began to slowly lose fullness
And started to fall featherlike
Easing its way toward the ground drifting
Coming in on an angle and sliding across the slick floor
Both of us spinning round in circles
As the note slowly faded from beneath me gone
And I found myself still sitting on the marble floor
Eyes closed and ears waiting to grab hold of the next note
That was coming my way
To have myself another ride
For I love where the music takes me

Lake Pontchartrain Daydream

I singed my legs on the August hot seawall bricks
While sitting there that stagnant summer afternoon
And after finger flicking away
A bead of sweat from my nose tip
Causing the only ripple on a slick wet lake
I watched the motionless trees wilt while
The entire day was paralyzed by heat and stillness
And I could only sit there thinking
Thinking of the wind
That must have left town earlier that day
Taking a vacation I supposed
Breezing off to a faraway place
While I could only imagine it
The wind swimming ashore
Atop the clear blue water
Spreading itself out stretched across
Some tropical beach somewhere
To dance with palm trees swaying
An island girl's hair tossed
While I sat there sweating
Tomorrow's conference calls
And endless bored meetings
Wishing I'd taken the ride
Gone with him on his trip
Cooling my toes in the ocean
Vacationing somewhere

With the wind
Laughing in my face

Resurrection of the Rain

With all he had
And all of his might
The sole raindrop tried
To hold onto the sky
Until his grip was torn away
And he plunged headlong
The body of him falling heavily
Crashing down
Dashed upon the sun splashed rocks below
And I watched
As the soul of him
In visions of steam
Evaporated before my eyes
Witnessing his ascension
Reborn
Back to the sky

Meeting a So Called Woman in Oz

She was a riddle in six-inch heels
A question
Mark
That punctured the mystery
With a sharp exclamation
Point
Then I heard the air escape
Deflating
The evening

Hate Consumes Itself

My memory's belly
Touches its backbone
As it is starved
For a good thought

Summer Morning in New Orleans

When you wake up
To a walk down Chartres Street
Summer morning in New Orleans
Comes in as a sticky curtain
Hanging down from the sky
Set adrift in the air
To envelop you
Like an invisible sheet
Wrapped round
Clinging wet
To your body and soul
As though you were
Walking through a fog cloud
Or perhaps a dream
It could be either
For in New Orleans
They can be
One and the same

McKenzie's Bakery 6:59 A.M.

Waiting outside the sweet-shop
An inviting aroma loiters there
Standing right next to you
Like some olden day merchant
Handing out free samples
For your nose to taste

Running Out of Coffee

I tossed this morning out onto the concrete street
Breaking it open and spilling its contents
Spread out wide in front of me
Mapping out everything from now till noon
One inch equals one minute you know
But I decided to stay in
This morning being too tough to navigate
Without help

Little Things at St. Alphonsus

As a skeptical schoolchild
I heard them speak of gamma rays
Molecules and quarks
Bacteria and miracles
But I'd never seen them
Not even one
So when questioning their truth
I was told to have a little faith
And so I did
Declaring the religion of science
Knowing that even though I couldn't see them
I had to believe that they were there
It was only right
And why not
Because I've always had a little faith
Which I can't see either

Treats on a Planetarium Visit

Quarter moon that night
The evening of my sixth birthday
Looking like a big scoop
Dipping into the sky
Picking up bits of stars
Sprinkled on ice cream galaxy swirls
And fed to my young mind
Giving me that headache you get
When tying to eat something
Too cold too fast

Waitin' at a Bus Stop

I was just sittin' there
Waitin' on the General Meyer bus when
Right behind me this afternoon
Was the Touro Shakespeare Home
Where I listened at the old black man
Sittin' cane in hand out front
Tears pooled on his bottom lid
Watchin' his son drive away
From his scheduled fifteen-minute visit
And heard him remark to his friend
"Put me here like I'm waitin' to die!"
To which his friend replied
"I got news for ya, from day one, we all waitin' to die!"
Which got me to thinkin'
Seems we always waitin' for something or another
At gas stations or in movie theatres traffic
Grocery stores and red lights
We do a lot of waitin' in this lifetime
That's why I don't mind so much waitin' anymore
Cause when it comes to waitin' on the bus
Or waitin' to die
I have infinite patience for both

Prosperity is Right Around the Corner

Old man Franklin was a card playin' fool
Never saw him take a pot but he still kept a playin'
He was always just this close but always one card shy
So there we all was that blazing hot Saturday night
Smoking some illegal Cubans and dealing five card
When old man Franklin up and keels over dead just like
that
Still clutchin' them cards in his right hand fingers
Which by the way was a straight flush hearts
First winnin' hand he ever had in his life
Least ways the first one that anybody at the table knew of
And ain't that just like old man Franklin to die like he lived
Just this close to cashing in his chips

Clumsy Love

She walked around square headed
Bumping into life
Scraping up against it
Too shy to look up

So I came to guide her
Keeping the path clear
Until she could smooth down the edges
And glide easily through the world

Random Affection

You pursed your lips and puckered
Then softly blew into the wand
Creating a shiny bubble loose
Floating across the room
Gently popping against my cheek
Delivering a wet soapy kiss

Ruby's Husband

I liked her just fine
But she gave me love
Which I did not want to take
Now she loves another
Who is always angry
I think it's because he knows
That some of his love is missing

Gone But Forgotten

I put out imaginary paper flyers
Stapled onto make-believe lamp posts
That line the endless hazy streets
In a forgotten part of my mind
On them are printed a shadowy picture
And contain a vague description
Of someone I used to know
Someone who still walks those streets
Wandering lost
Somewhere in my memory

Hummingbirds at Audubon Park

On his air perch invisible
Iridescent blue face
Dangling from a glass string
Or hanging by a clear hook
Then flying like a dart
Using daisies black centers as bull's-eyes
Playing his carefree game
And lunching in the flowerbed
Humming a tune
All the words since lost
While gathering nectar and pleasure
From honeysuckles and sunny afternoons
Then moving on
To have another take its place
Iridescent red face
With a playful fire in his humming tune
But continuing the same little melody
Picked up where the blue face left off
And wouldn't you just know it
They know the same song
Even with all the words since lost

The Lone Tree

On a summer day of storms
Through the back porch window
One could peer out at
The lone tree
Standing upon the hill
Silhouetted for a moment
By the darkening clouds
The tree stood listening
Listening to the thunder that was
Running in its direction
Hammering feet
Stomping their way across the sky floor
Growing closer always
Until its lightning foot
Slipped off the edge of a cloud
And came down hard
Stamping out the tree
Then went running away
Chased by
Traces of rolling laughter
Rippling through the clouds
But the lone tree
Would have the last laugh
For you see
It had died
Many years ago
Having lived

A much fuller life
Than would the storm

Games Before a Rain

Looking up toward the bright sky
Squinting, I closed my eyes
And then the sun hid itself
Behind some gray clouds
As a shy child would do
Until I slightly opened my eyes again
To catch it peeking at me
While I was peeking back

Algiers Field of Clover

From the bosom of the meadow
A field of clover nod
Hello to the passing wind
Three leaves all
Pulled themselves up
Together the same
The same that is but one
Carrying leaves that numbered four
Carefully blending
Within the others
Leading me to question
Is it hiding from shame of difference
Or held different in esteem
Protected
Disguised by the admiring crowd

Passing an Afternoon With the River

We drank from the clear river cool
Then swam fun in it
Taking that pleasure for ourselves
And later that evening
We fished the river
And fried them on the bank

We took so much from the river
And never once did it stop or complain
But instead moved on and along with its life flowing
Leaving bits of itself with each of us along the bank
Never missing what it gave
Just as we hope to do in each other's lives… the same

A Day in New Orleans is Like…

Taking a world cruise on a drop of water
Or containing a forest fire inside of a matchbox
Or holding a parade in your pocket
Or having a circus in your closet
Or giving a huge party in a dollhouse

Early Morning Grass at Woldenberg Park

When chilly night descends upon the schoolyard
Blades of grass slip into hoarfrost coats
And stay huddled together for warmth
Jealous of the temperate leaves
Chasing after the wind in fun while
They stand breathlessly waiting to see the face
Of the autumn morning sun
Their friend who comes nearly every day
With long arms and warm hands
To help them shed their clothing
So they too can take recess
With the wind

Thanksgiving at Julie and Roger's

We came to the old Coliseum house
Renewed despite the neighbors petty pecking
Came on this crisp breaking cold Thursday
Our hellos to each other bent sideways by the wind
Then went inside to warm hearts and kisses
And sat together to partake of delicious food and words
Spilled out across a rich and glad table
Conversation covered in thick gravy
Then washed down with good red wine
I sopped up every wonderful morsel I could
Until my head and belly were stuffing full
And left stumbling over recollections revealed
That were strewn about the floor
For my ears to pick up on my way out
My thoughts now soaked to a mellow drunk
I bid farewell to our kind hosts
Happy for the ride home to a soft bed and wife
And thankful for great friends and strangers alike

Pretending

I tried my hand at acting
But I wasn't very good
At trying to act natural
So that night
While contemplating my failure
I starred at the wooden cabinets
Across the dimly lit room
The wood grain was perfect
Circles and curves
Lines of pure natural artistry
Years in the making
Spoke to me
Until I realized
That it wasn't wood at all
But actually plastic that looked like wood
Which made me laugh because
Even plastic was a better actor
Than I

Jealousy Blinds the Artist

He could no longer see
Because his eyes were trained
On you
Constantly searching for cracks
Or perhaps a seam
In the flawless white
Porcelain glass cloud
He had created
And placed around you
Encased you in
To watch and wait
For a glancing blow
From another's eyes
To shatter his illusion
But only
As far as he could see

A Painting of Shirley

The portrait is there
Lying on the table
As yet unseen
But it is there
Hidden inside the paints
Paints that cover the palette
The picture concealed
All of its parts
The eyes, the hands, the expression
Lie there in the form
Of separate small colored globs
Waiting to be assembled
By the artists skilled hands

Oliver

He slips over the border crossed
Right under our very eyes
Thinking his humanity is evident
To everyone that knows him
That wanting humanity
Hiding behind steely blue eyes
Counting on his quickness
Knowing me to be an easy mark
He looks strong and confident
Peering at me from the other side of the room
Trying to stare me down
As he often does to those people
Who know his true character
Bringing me to numbness
All the while relying on the coolness of this movements
As he slides methodically into position
Poised to strike
Lunging forward suddenly
When his cadence changes
And weakness appears
To overtake him
As he lies down seemingly defeated
To begin purring in my lap

The Trouble With Bob

I drag my troubles behind me
Connected as a long string of rolling weights
Adding more weight with every day
All trying to slow down my life

But when I look back
Over my shoulder

I realize that they're all behind me
Which in my mind
Makes it easier
To push ahead

Tuesday Night at the Crown and Anchor

We talked of the sea the old man and I
Through whiskey shots and cigar smoke fog
His leather face a taut mask with deep set eyes
We spoke of how much she missed him
The sea being his mistress and all
Of how she was there waiting for him
Down there at the waterfront
Waiting for him to return to her arms
The arms he had left long ago for wanting
Her to remember him the way he was
Fair haired and bright eyes strong
Not with hands of parchment skin
Stretched tight across spokes of bone
He talked of her with longing regrets
As he could never return to the sea
His waning heart so heavy with age
That no ship would dare take him on hand
For fear of sinking under its weight

Deja Vu On a Barstool at Yvonne's Shooters

After the long today
When twilights curtain
Skirted the ground
I walked round behind it
To the other side of this thin day
And looked back through it transparent
Seeing a moment in time
As it is now and has been before
Gazing at pictures of fading life
Spied through dwindling light
Until the curtain eventually fell
Covering me in darkness
Though it lasted for only a second
But long enough
To live this moment again
Just as I had seen it
Through twilights curtain

What We Think At 21 and 31 and 41 and 51

We were all so young
How could we know

We were all so smart
How could we not know

And even now
When we all seem so old

We still
Do not know

Hidden Wishes of the Cynic's Son or The Gravity of the Situation

My whole life
They always said
Try to stay grounded
But I always wanted
To take the leap

To freefall…

Just once

But they liked to remind me
That nothing is really free
That everything will fall
And that the ground is always there
For you to never leave
Or for you to slam into

Eating my Words

I have toiled with hammer and nail
With fire and water to earn my pay
Now I wish to trade words for wages
Exchange syllables for my supper
But I suspect that poetry will be
Just another helpful dietary aid

www.ingramcontent.com/pod-product-compliance
Ingram Content Group UK Ltd.
Pitfield, Milton Keynes, MK11 3LW, UK
UKHW041846190726
13854UKWH00002B/736